THE GUADALUPES

by
Dan Murphy

GUADALUPE MOUNTAINS NATIONAL PARK

© 1984
Carlsbad Caverns • Guadalupe Mountains
Association
3225 National Parks Highway
Carlsbad, New Mexico 88220

ISBN No. 0-916907-00-7

On October 15, 1966, the Congress of the United States passed legislation "to provide for the establishment of the Guadalupe Mountains National Park in the State of Texas . . . in order to preserve in public ownership an area . . . possessing outstanding geological values together with scenic and other natural values of great significance."

That was far away in Washington, D. C.

Out here in the park-to-be the wind blew through the ponderosas up in The Bowl, squirrels skittered through the autumn leaves in McKittrick Canyon, and the sun baked the desert flats. The bill in Congress did not seem to make much difference; yet with passage of the act came protection for a mountain range that contained the Capitan Reef, the most famous fossil reef in the world; a fragile relict forest; a classic desert mountain range; and a hundred thousand plants and animals, large and small, quite unaware that anything had happened at all. The nation

had decided that this was a place so special that it should be set aside to be enjoyed by its citizens. Since then many have come to hike, to study, to work, or simply to view the great mountain. The National Park Service continues to study the range and to help visitors understand the uniqueness of the place. This book is meant to convey some of the knowledge, and some of the experience, of Guadalupe Mountains National Park.

LYNN A. NYMEYER

MICHAEL ALLENDER

CATHY J. RUDY

Awesome El Capitan stands as a famous landmark in the Gualalupe Mountains, but the visitor should take a closer look. In its shadow are a thousand lesser known details: a butterfly; autumn leaf litter on the floor of Pine Spring Canyon; and a blooming prickly pear cactus.

ONCE IT WAS OCEAN

Once it was ocean. It is hard to imagine now, with cactus poking through the parched soil and with no open water as far as the eye can see. But 250 million years ago this region was an arm of the Permian Ocean, and that fact is responsible for the existence of the Guadalupe Mountains.

We can be quite sure of much of what we say about the Guadalupes, for it is one of the most studied mountain ranges in the world. At first, through mere curiosity, scientists tried to determine how things came to be as they are. Half a century ago, however, as world demand for petroleum grew,

it gradually became apparent that understanding the geology of the Guadalupes might lead to discovery of the sources and location of oil, not only in this region but perhaps elsewhere in the world. Scientists—from universities, government surveys, and oil companies—have been studying the geology of the Guadalupe Mountains ever since. To them these mountains have gradually yielded some, but not all, of their secrets.

An early recognized secret was that once an ocean was here. In Permian times a deep, tri-lobed arm

Previous pages: Looking down over El Capitan from Guadalupe Peak.

Most of the 400-mile-long Capitan Reef lies buried, but in three mountain ranges—The Guadalupe, Apache and Glass Mountains—it stands above the surrounding plains as high as 4000 feet.

MILES
0 ———————— 50

The reef grew both laterally and upward, as determined by water conditions which created a favorable home for lime-secreting organisms.

The fore reef is made up of loose material from the top of the reef that rolled down the steep slope into the basin and joined with sedimentary material from the sea.

The Capitan Reef or reef massive is a non-layered formation made up of skeletal remains of plant and animal organisms and calcium carbonate that precipitated from the ocean water.

The back reef deposits are layered sediments.

of the ocean reached up from the south like the triple leaves of poison ivy. Its center lobe, which stretched from near present-day Alpine, Texas, northwestward to shoals near the present-day Guadalupe Mountains, is known as the Delaware Basin. (Readers may have heard of the Permian Basin. This is a geologist's term for the entire west Texas-southeast New Mexico area, of which the Delaware Basin is a part.) Of course, there were no humans here, nor anywhere in the world, but by assembling evidence from beneath microscopes in Houston and Tulsa, from core drillings that oil field roughnecks bring from deep in the ground, and from the discoveries of graduate students who swarm over the mountains with their notebooks and hand lenses, we can roughly reconstruct what a Permian explorer would have seen.

From the highlands of New Mexico, say around present-day Albuquerque, heading southeastward toward Texas, this imaginary explorer would have traveled down a long gradual slope of sand and clay. This was an alluvial plain, the result of rains slowly eroding the high country

and moving the debris southward toward the ocean. After days of land travel, he would have smelled the ocean breezes as one does today nearing a coast. Finally broad tidal flats, tens of miles wide, came into view—no motels, no highways, just the flats. When the tide was in, the flats were covered with a few feet of water; at low tide they were reduced to mud and glistening tidal pools. There seems to have been no sharp division where the tidal flats deepened to a broad, shallow lagoon. We know much about this lagoon. For instance, it generally was neither fresh water nor normal ocean water. Instead it was heavy with mineral salts that had been concentrated as lagoon water evaporated. At times layers of sand extended across it.

On the ocean side, a shoal separated the lagoon from the deeper open waters of the basin. The shoal was sometimes awash and sometimes slightly submerged. At times when sea level was a bit lower, it may have been a line of low islands. Only a few miles wide, this shoal effectively restricted circulation between the lagoon and the open ocean.

Beyond the shoal the bottom of the ocean sloped away. For perhaps a half mile or more the slope was gradual. Then it became much steeper as it descended to depths of about 1,500 feet where it flattened out on the floor of the Delaware Basin. The profile of this slope resembled the profile of a ski jump. Of critical importance to geologists, different rocks formed at different places along the slope. The Capitan Reef, the most famous of the rocks formed on this profile, developed at the upper part just where the curve steepened into the basin. The Capitan Reef was not a surf zone or barrier reef like those of South Sea islands today. It was a type of reef with no apparent modern counterpart. The reef formed here in part because along this upper slope thrived many types of marine organisms, the most abundant of which were sponges which secreted lime skeletons. (Modern reefs are composed largely of corals.) In addition to sponges, many other tiny animals and plants (algae) also secreted lime. Generation after generation of organisms donated their skeletons to the growing reef mass. In addition, a large amount of lime was precipitated inorganically from the ocean water. This coated and cemented the skeletons and other sea-floor sediment.

JEFF RENNICKE

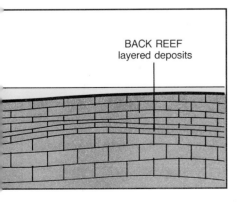

BACK REEF
layered deposits

The reef revealed. Softer seabed sediments have eroded away, leaving the harder rock of the reef. View southwest from near Carlsbad Caverns National Park.

Fossil shells like these, glimpsed in rocks along the trails in the Guadalupe Mountains, remind us of earlier life here.

The amount of inorganic calcium carbonate that precipitated from the water in places greatly exceeded the amount provided by organisms. This precipitate, a secret discovered only recently, is a distinctive feature of the Capitan Reef.

Our imaginary explorer, of course, saw the lagoon shoal and ocean basin complex as it was at a particular moment in its million years of formation. Actually, the earth was no more static then than it is now. While the reef grew its limestone, in front and behind it other sediments (carbonates, sand and evaporites) were forming different rock layers just as important, though not as famous, as the Capitan Reef. Today it is a complex mosaic, and understanding it is a challenge and a triumph for curiosity.

But even oceans are only temporary. Perhaps 200 million years ago the connection between the Delaware Basin and the ocean was partially closed. The now-inland sea began to evaporate. As the water became saltier, the lime-secreting organisms died. The change was rapid in geologic terms, perhaps not even as long as a million years. As the water of the Delaware Basin evaporated, tremendous amounts of calcium sulfate (gypsum) and later, sodium chloride (halite or table salt) were deposited, filling the basin. Millions of years later some of these beds also would be found to contain potassium salts which today are mined at nearby Carlsbad.

Opposite: Layered sedimentary rock revealed by stream erosion.

Water follows and enlarges cracks in limestone. Sometimes tree roots—here those of an alligator juniper—follow the cracks.

As the basin dried up, sediment continued to collect, gradually covering all evidence of the Permian ocean. Time passed, different animals evolved and walked on the earth's surface or flew above it, then became extinct. The reef and the sediments that had gathered around it were buried thousands of feet deep. Heat and pressure gradually made them into sandstone, limestone, and evaporites. Though they were changed, they still carried clues of what they had once been.

Under pressure and gentle heat, organic matter from the billions of small marine creatures, which once teemed in the Delaware Basin, slowly changed. The carbon and hydrogen and oxygen of those creatures slowly cooked and were converted into microscopic droplets of gas and oil. Some of these gathered in traps of porous rock. (One day another species would find uses for this black liquid and gas, first because it burned, then because of other properties: it could become anything from nylon fabrics, to lubricants, to long-playing records. It would warm homes, fuel industries, and propel vehicles.)

The huge reef system that had once nearly surrounded the Delaware Basin lay buried, a giant limestone bracelet around the ancient basin, cushioned in a setting of sediment.

In a much later geologic period, merely ten million years or so before the present, a period of uplifting began throughout the western United States. For the traveler coming from the plains of west Texas the Guadalupes are one of the first of these uplifted ranges encountered, the beginning of a succession of such ranges reaching through Nevada. Whole blocks were uplifted while adjacent blocks slumped downward. The Permian shelf/basin complex, including what had been the land, the sediments of the lagoon, the reef, and the ancient basin, were raised. As always, forces immediately began tearing them down. Each raindrop carried an infinitesimal portion of the uplifted mountain block a little way toward the sea. The sedimentary rocks on the basin side were softer than the limestone reef, so they were stripped away faster. Imagine time-lapse photography, slowed to geologic time. With one exposure

each thousand years, the reef slowly emerges. The basin sediments began to erode even as they appeared, but the reef majestically remained to stand in the air as it had once stood in the water.

Most viewers see only the southeast edge of the Guadalupe Mountains where the highway now passes. But to the geologist, and to those who simply feel excitement and awe in seeing the rugged face of a mountain, the western escarpment presents a fascinating panorama. This is the break, in geologic terms a fault, where the block containing the reef and its associated rock layers slowly moved upwards, the block to the west downwards. Today it is an abrupt 4,000-foot rise, and there is evidence that the movement is continuing. Here magnificent rock exposures record many millions of years of geologic history, culminating in the thousand-foot vertical cliffs below El Capitan and Guadalupe, Shumard and Bartlett peaks. All of these show evidence of the steep slopes on which the Capitan limestone grew and the downward transition into gentle slopes at the edge of the basin where limestone gives way to the less resistant sandstones of the basin floor.

The mountain erodes not only on the outside but on the inside too. Limestone dissolves, especially in water that is slightly acidic. Rainwater, charged with carbon dioxide from the air, becomes an extremely dilute carbonic acid that commonly becomes more acidic as it passes through soil. Through the ages this water seeped into the limestone, following a rectangular crack pattern in the rock. As it worked its way through the cracks, which geologists call joints, it dissolved the limestone, forming caverns in the rock. Nobody knows how many caves have formed in the ancient limestone reef, for usually only those that open to the surface are discovered. At least 200 are known, and some are huge: magnificent Carlsbad Cavern is one, occurring in the same fossil reef that forms the backbone of the Guadalupe Mountains. (Carlsbad Caverns National Park is about 35 miles northeast of Guadalupe Mountains National Park.) The larger rooms of Carlsbad Cavern developed in the Capitan Reef formation. Because of the way the reef was formed, its rock is not in layers. Therefore, huge arched caverns could develop in it without the roof collapsing.

It is an easy misconception to think that the great earth movements have ceased. Sometimes, unconsciously, we think that the whole point of geologic change was simply to make things as they are now. This mistake is borne of man's brief lifespan. The geologic time scale so dwarfs the mere eighty years or so allotted to humans that change seems imperceptible to us. But sit at one of the tables in Pine Springs Campground and look north. Let your eyes become accustomed to the great cliff, the boulders that have rolled down it, the patterns of the colors. Now do you see it, the bottom half of an hourglass shape that is wide at the bottom and narrowing toward the top? Probably centuries old, that is a tiny victory for gravity in its fight to pull the mountain down.

It is the debris of a landslide. It must have been a noisy, tremendous event, and as the thunder died away the dust went floating out over the west Texas desert. How many animals and plants died, their remains buried beneath the debris for years, slowly to be incorporated into the mountain? The jumbled debris of the slide is of a different density and texture than that of the rest of the slope. Water moves through it differently, and therefore it supports a slightly different plant community. That is why its overall color is different. Apparently water and soil collect at the edges of the old slide. The green borders show where a few more trees have managed to take root and thrive.

This is the stuff of geology. Every event leaves its mark: the existence of an ocean 200 million years ago, the creatures which swam in it, the water drops which seeped through the limestone, and now the earth in its unimaginably slow churning bringing the mountain down. Any pebble, any grain of sand that moves in the rain ends up slightly lower than where it started. The Guadalupe Mountains are a magnificent monument to the unfolding history of the earth and the curiosity of passing humans to know how things come to be as they are.

Water makes the difference. Water carved beautiful McKittrick Canyon, and the presence of water in the canyon today makes possible its stand of hardwood trees.

UNEXPECTED VARIETY

Previous pages: Clouds forming over the Guadalupes.

Opposite: Prickly pear cactus and Texas madrone tree.

At one time all of the Guadalupe range and the desert around it were covered with sediment and rock. Then the rock was uplifted and exposed to the forces of erosion which immediately began the long, slow process of wearing it all down to sea level again. But something else happened too. Imagine again the immensely slow time-lapse movies of the range emerging. The bare rock did not rear up suddenly from the ground. If our Permian explorer had somehow returned to see this event, he probably would not have noticed any single point of the change. An imperceptible tilt developed in the ground, centimeters in a century. The earth rose, it paused a few thousand years, it rose again. Plants that had lived successfully at one elevation gradually failed to reproduce when the elevation was higher and the temperatures probably cooler.

Even as this new mountain range emerged, constantly changing life spread over it. Picture a thin, green, interconnected web, lacing

over the range and finding any nook or cranny on which to grow. Lichens began breaking down rock, the first step in the making of life-sustaining soil. Small plants established footholds where they could and insects came to feed on them, and aided in pollination at the same time. Seeds were carried by birds, by the wind, by clinging with burrhooks to traveling animals. Most seeds fell in unsuitable places and became food for something else; but a few—enough—fell where they could grow. Larger plants clung where soil and water were adequate. The web is infinitely complex, and biologists who study the park are quick to explain that they are barely scratching the surface.

Contrary to many people's idea of the desert, there is not too little water here. There is just the right amount for a desert, and plants and animals have adapted to what is available. Cacti offer the most famous example of adaptation to the desert, and in a short stroll anywhere in the lower elevations of the park the visitor will find plenty of them. The cholla (CHOY-ya) are among the most beautiful, but among the most wicked too. Their leaves have been reduced to spines, decreasing the surface area from which they lose water.

D.A. BUEHLER

CATHY J. RUDY

LYNN A. NYMEYER

ponderosa pine

Texas madrone fruit

horse crippler cactus

New Mexico agave

LAURENCE PARENT

(The common idea that spines protect cactus from grazers may have some truth, but they do not seem to bother some animals. Wood rats merrily eat and build nests in the cholla.) Like that of any cactus, the cholla's root system is a marvel of design, gathering water quickly after infrequent desert showers. Also helpful for a plant in such a harsh environment is the cholla's self-pruning ability. Its branches are in segments, like a string of sausages. In a severe drought the outer segments dry and drop off, reducing both the plant's surface area and its need for water. This is why it is so wicked for humans, and why one species is called "jumping" cholla. The outer, loosely connected pieces easily cling to anything or anyone who bumps into them. The cholla has striking magenta pink, waxy blossoms, and a single plant may display hundreds of flowers.

Many of the smaller cacti, pincushions and various mammillaria for example, are obscure on the desert floor and are likely to be missed by even the most observant eye. But wait until the blossoms come! Then, to attract the insects necessary for pollination, the plants produce flowers in a startling variety of bright pinks, purples, reds, and oranges.

A desert plant often mistaken for a cactus is the agave, but agaves are succulents. The wide, thick leaves of the agave have needle-sharp points, and a chemical on the end produces an unpleasant chill that seems to go right up your arm if you prick yourself with one.

The larger species of agave are called "century plants" because of their long life cycles. Storing up energy for a decade or two, the plant finally shoots up a large central seed stalk in just a few days. After it flowers and produces seeds, the plant dies. The heart of this agave or mescal plant was used for food by Indians but not food only; fermented mescal sap makes the intoxicating drink of the same name.

A smaller agave, lechuguilla (lay-chu-GHEE-ah), is very common in the park. Though not as spectacular as the larger species, it was equally useful, especially for the fabric that the Indians made from the leaf fibers.

Yuccas are sometimes mistaken for cacti too, but they are members of the lily family. Another member of the lily family, the sotol, was also an important source of food for the Apache. It is difficult for the modern visitor, for whom desert plants are only interesting oddities, to realize the many uses Indians had for them. Yucca root, for instance, can produce a soap, and the Indians also knew the plant's medicinal properties.

Animals that live in the low desert country share the same need as the plant—water. They too must know how to find it, keep it, or get along without much of it. Sometimes their solutions are simple. Deer are common here, but they are seldom seen in the hot part of the day. They avoid the burning, moisture-requiring sun and come out at dusk and are often seen by visitors near watering places. Smaller mammals have made similar adaptations, remaining in cool underground burrows during

mule deer

faxon yucca

NATIONAL PARK SERVICE

MICHAEL ALLENDER

the day and coming out at night to seek food. Astonishingly, some desert rodents get along with no drinking water at all, synthesizing it instead from carbohydrates in the seeds they eat.

Coyotes are common. Campers will enjoy their concerts but seldom see them, since they hunt the ubiquitous rabbits and rodents at night.

For many people reptiles are the very symbol of the desert. Snakes, being cold-blooded, do not need to spend energy keeping their body at any particular temperature; thus they eat much less than one would expect. This is an advantage in the desert, a sparsely set table at best. The visitor is fortunate to see a snake because besides being shy, they avoid the burning sun and move about mostly at night.

Lizards, distant cousins of the snakes, function in the daytime. They shift from shade to sun and back again to regulate their body temperature, then they sit motionless for long periods, waiting for an unwary insect to come within reach of their lightning-fast tongue. Even sitting stone-still, they are totally alert.

One need not list the hundreds of species of plants and animals that have adjusted to life in the desert to appreciate the complexity of desert ecology. Each of them, in one way or another, lives off the others in an interdependence we are just beginning to understand. A handbook, a canteen, patience, and a short walk can introduce a person to fascinating discoveries in the natural world.

Marvelous though the desert is, it is only part of the uniqueness of Guadalupe Mountains National Park. Very special are the unexpected corners of life borne of this range's special history and location. The Guadalupes are on the edge of several "life-zones." Texas madrone trees here are at the northern edge of their range, Douglas-fir are at the extreme southern ends of theirs, and eastern Chinquapin oak are found as far west as they grow. In fact, twelve plants and six animals in the park are considered rare for this region. Scientists believe that a few thousand years ago, when the climate was wetter and cooler, these now-rare plants and animals may have been common in the forests which extended into the region. As conditions began to dry, the forests retreated, but high in the cooler, more moist Guadalupes relict stands were left behind.

porcupine

sotol

black-tailed rattlesnake

Other special places are the springs, the wonders of the park. Smith Spring, Manzanita Spring . . . any place where water emerges in the desert it attracts and supports an abundance of life. Easy hikes to these low-country places are among the most rewarding in the park. One of the most special (and famous) is McKittrick Canyon. It is surprising indeed to find a running stream in the desert, but the real bonus is the wealth of life along it. Though a walk into McKittrick begins in desert, soon the plants multiply and the visitor sees species which may be familiar from hundreds of miles away. Here are the broad-leafed plants of a wetter climate, oaks and maples, and in autumn the canyon can be a riot of color.

The unexpected variety of plants in the watered places is matched by the animal life. Deer are here, and also mountain lions, bobcats, the shy ringtail cats, foxes, even black bears. This is no barren desert! Birds flit from tree to tree (more than forty species nest in McKittrick Canyon). To protect this fragile beauty, only day hikes are permitted in the canyon.

The unexpected biological find of the Guadalupes is the high country. Here also is relict forest, left from wetter times. Among the aspens, firs and pines wander the birds and animals one expects to find in a forest much farther north.

A few numbers may tell the story. Park checklists show birds—225 species; mammals—67; amphibians and reptiles—58; and insects—11,000 species, merely providing a "working nucleus" for future efforts. The desert mountain range is not empty. It is subtle, balanced, changing, and fascinating.

CATHY J. RUDY

Opposite: Smith Spring, where water created a hidden oasis in the desert.

mescal bean blossom

Water supports lush growth in McKittrick Canyon.

MICHAEL ALLENDER

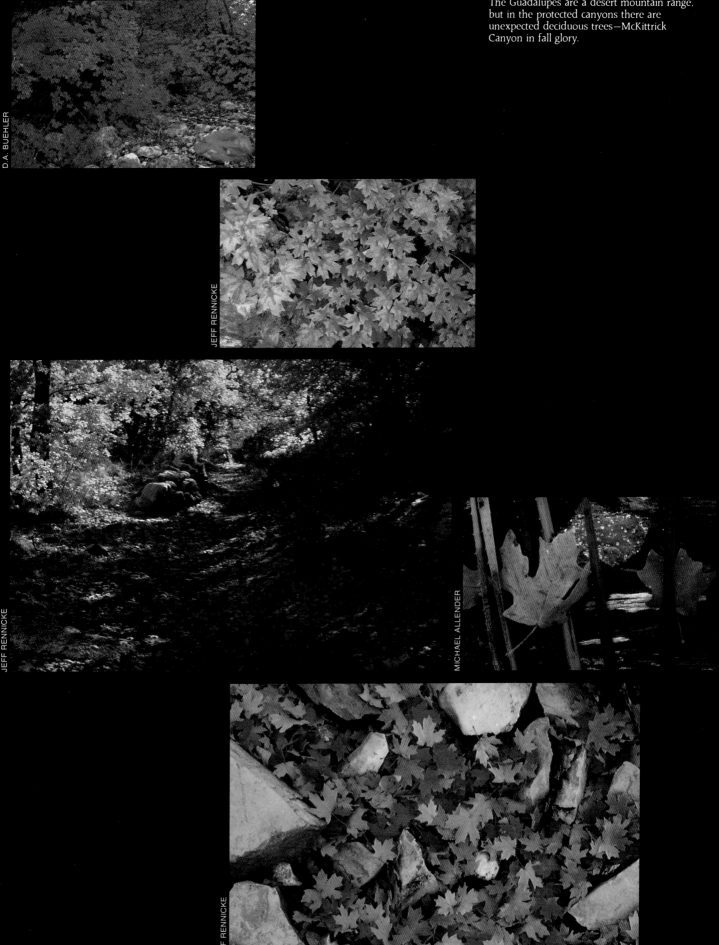

The Guadalupes are a desert mountain range, but in the protected canyons there are unexpected deciduous trees—McKittrick Canyon in fall glory.

D.A. BUEHLER

JEFF RENNICKE

JEFF RENNICKE

MICHAEL ALLENDER

JEFF RENNICKE

MAN IN THE GUADALUPES

We cannot think with the mind of the person who first saw the Guadalupes. We do not know his language, his religion, or what he thought of the range. That first wanderer and his band may have been hunting camels or four-horned antelope, both extinct now. When they saw the distant outline of the Guadalupes, they must have known there would be water and different plants at this high place; perhaps they had come to find them. Later someone stayed for a while in a shelter, and archeologists have found what was left behind—projectile points, baskets, pottery. The remains date to about 12,000 years ago. We do not know much more about those first visitors save this—they had the skills to exist in a formidable situation.

Much, much later a different group of Indians used the resources of the Guadalupes, the famous Apaches. They were nomads, often hunting buffalo and traveling great distances even though they did not have horses. Recognizing the variety of resources a mountain range brings to the desert, they came at various times of the year to find the fruits of cactus and the nuts of the piñon, to hunt in the high country, and to rest in places made luxurious by water. When hiking on a park trail, look away from the trail and imagine an Apache walking in the hills. Look a few yards to the side where no trail crew has been; that is what the Apaches moved through! Occasionally hikers come across stone circles, often mistaking them for tipi rings. Apaches did live in leather tipis, or sometimes brush "jacales," but these stone circles have nothing to do with those dwellings. These were roasting pits for agave or mescal. The Apaches would harvest the large hearts of the plants with their tremendous amount of stored starch and roast great quantities of them in these pits. It was a major food source for them, hence the name Mescalero Apache.

But change is as inevitable in human societies as in geology, and it is usually faster. First came rumors of strangers, or maybe a few of the Apaches ranging in the Guadalupes actually saw the four ragged men who came by, parading as medicine men but actually survivors of a Spanish shipwreck on the Gulf coast. Word soon came from the Apaches' trading partners up in the Rio Grande valley that a remarkable army, of unprecedented strength and ferocity, had arrived. The year was A.D. 1540; the army was Coronado's. The Apaches' life would never be the same, as their old trading relationships broke down. But apparently no Spaniards actually entered the Guadalupes or explored the area.

Opposite: Thrusting high, the Guadalupes often intercept moisture from the clouds. Early hunters knew mountains would have resources the desert lacked.

New Mexico agave, food source for Mescalaero Apaches.

MICHAEL ALLENDER

Although the isolation of the Guadalupes lasted a long time, it was impossible for it to be permanent. A young, rambunctious country born on the East Coast began spreading westward with explosive energy. Army detachments sent out by the young United States to find routes to and through the West soon saw the dramatic outline of the Guadalupes, with magnificent El Capitan standing guard at its southern end. In 1849 Captain Randolph Marcy correctly deduced that there would be springs at the foot of the mountain, and his company found them. In fact, that was a wet year and Marcy reported that the area was lush. The lushness was only temporary, and others soon realized it as they struggled with weakening animals over the desert. They found brief relief at the dependable springs before striking out again, some for failure and death.

Still the United States would not give up or even slow its expansion. Gold had been discovered on the West Coast and a new state called California was booming; the country needed to connect its two coasts. In 1857 a private businessman, John Butterfield, won a contract to tie the country together with his overland stage. He was granted 320 acres for each changing station and built one near Pine Springs. Now El Capitan

saw history; on September 25, 1858, the first westbound stage met the first eastbound stage on the desert beneath El Capitan. For almost a year an occasional stage lumbered by, making its noisy, dusty, swaying way over Guadalupe Pass, the drivers knowing they had now crossed the highest point on the route. But the hard facts of the Guadalupe environment were making themselves felt, as were the Apaches. Soon the stage route was changed to a safer, better watered one farther south.

The Apaches, realizing at last that this new invasion was a direct threat to their homeland, had begun to act. The Guadalupes, long their home, now became their refuge. They fought with the newcomers, then retreated to the mountains, where for years the army did not care to follow. But finally even that changed. For the first time, war came to the Guadalupes.

On the day after Christmas in 1869 the terrifying noise of gunfire shattered the peace of one of the canyons of the Guadalupes, possibly McKittrick Canyon, as an army unit under Lieutenant H. B. Cushing surprised an Apache camp. He reported destroying over ten tons of mescal root, leaving the Apaches without food for the winter. A few days later another fight broke out near Manzanita Spring, a peaceful place where visitors stroll today. For years there were such occasional encounters, and cavalry stations were established near springs within the present boundaries of the national park. Geronimo knew these mountains and so did Victorio. But by 1880 it was over. The Mescalero Apaches were a memory with their name attached to a reservation miles to the northwest, and the Guadalupes were open for the new settlers to make of them what they could.

Manzanita Spring, site of tragic cavalry attack on a Mescalero Indian winter camp in 1869.

Which was not much. A few settlers established ranches around the base of the range, and the hiker who comes across the remains of one today cannot help but be moved. Some weather-beaten boards or a rocked-up spring speak eloquently of someone who braved isolation and hardships beyond today's standards. Undoubtedly there were cheery, good times in those houses along with the weariness and the worry, but the area was still too dry and too isolated to be developed. Not deliberately, the land was being saved for other uses.

A new kind of rancher came in 1921, a young geologist named Wallace Pratt. In later years Pratt liked to tell of the time someone told him about the prettiest spot in Texas, and when he hiked into McKittrick Canyon, he decided that was the place. Pratt was no ordinary geologist. He recognized the significance of the Guadalupes by understanding the geology of the surrounding area and what this implied in the search for oil. His predictions were right; Humble Oil Company (now Exxon) grew on his insights and he became its vice president. Fascinated by McKittrick Canyon, Pratt bought up land in it. The canyon is a remarkable combination of beauty and geologic grandeur, being a textbook dissection of the most famous fossil reef in the world. High on the wall near the canyon entrance there is a particularly clear exposure cut across the junction of the ancient reef and the sediments lying against it. Below, along the road into the cabin that Pratt built in the canyon, there is a place nicknamed "the arm-waving spot." Rangers explain that Pratt often stopped here to show this special broad, cross-section view of the reef to the many geologists who came to visit, and it seems there was "just something about this spot that seemed to make geologists want to wave their arms around!" No doubt it was because so many geologic features could be pointed out from here.

This was perhaps the kind of ranching the Guadalupes could support, gentleman ranching, heavy with outside capital. Another such rancher came in, a judge and politician named J. C. Hunter, Sr. Buying small ranches that failed during the Depression, he created a large operation. His men labored long and hard laying a water line from the high country down Bear Canyon to a spring to provide water for a sheep operation. (The remains of that line are visible along the Bear Canyon Trail; the labor must have been awesome.) Like Pratt, Hunter was aware of the value of this land, and he tried early to find some way to preserve it. His son, J. C. Hunter, Jr., continued the same interest. The country owes much to these men. Pratt donated almost 6,000 acres to the National Park Service, and Congress responded in 1966 by authorizing Guadalupe Mountains National Park. Systematically other lands were bought, with special cooperation from J. C. Hunter, Jr., and in 1972 the park was dedicated.

Pratt's rock cabin, McKittrick Canyon.

Wallace E. Pratt, pioneer petroleum geologist and conservationist.

Rock walls are all that remain of the historic Butterfield Stage Stations.

CONGRESS SET IT ASIDE

Besides national park status, the Guadalupe Mountains received special protection in 1972 when Congress set aside 46,850 acres, about 60% of the park, as wilderness. Of course, it was wilderness before it was set aside—it was wilderness before there was a congress. Being designated as such means Congress recognized such facets as "the opportunity for solitude" and "untrammeled by man," and protects these wilderness virtues perpetually through management restraints. For expample, in a wilderness area hikers and campers my not use "mechanized equipment," and you'll never be startled by a nearby engine of some sort—nor will the animals who share the wilderness with you. Now in almost all of the park's high country, when the breeze blows through the fir trees and across the meadows, that's all you hear. In wilderness, you and I are the most delicate of guests. The philosophy of a national park, especially one containing wilderness, is that it be managed in as natural a state as possible. This is not as easy as it sounds, as man had already brought changes to the Guadalupes, some not easily reversed.

An example is the occurrence of forest fires. About 80 percent of the fires in the Guadalupes are caused by lightning, fires that have been happening for millenia, long before man began putting them out. Research has shown that over the last 300 years fires occurred about every seventeen years. In this relatively brief interval undergrowth and forest litter did not build up before the next fire; when fires did come, they were not tremendous. They were "normal" forest fires. With little forest litter to burn, the fires were "cool," and larger trees often escaped serious damage. But in historic times man began trying to suppress fires and, unfortunately, usually succeeded. As a result there has been such a buildup of fuel that when a fire does start it may be tremendous, much more harmful than the normal fires of past years. National Park Service scientists are studying this problem.

Managing an area to keep it natural seems like a contradiction, but it is a problem the National Park Service often faces. For example, Barbary sheep, an African species, live in the park. Some escaped from a private ranch in New Mexico and became established in the mountain range, an environment that apparently suits them. They do so well that they might be crowding out native species. As the Park Service philosophy is to have the mountain be as it would be without human interference, these sheep are an intrusion.

On the other hand, the Park Service may deliberately reintroduce native species that have disappeared for human-caused reasons. Cattle and sheep grazing drastically changed the range. Apparently they were responsible for the disappearance of bighorn sheep, which used to live here naturally, and of harlequin quail, because heavy grazing affected the plant cover. Now the cattle are gone and native vegetation is returning. In 1985 harlequin quail were reintroduced in the Dog Canyon area of the Guadalupes with some success. The Park Service hopes that with wise management in years to come park visitors will be able to see these animals at home in their mountain range.

There are no easy solutions to these and many other resource management problems. A giant stride has been made. The area is a national park. Congress set it aside, and now it belongs to all the American people, permanently. The range that once was an ocean is now a public park, an extraordinary outdoor laboratory.

Opposite: El Capitan

ON THE TRAIL

Starting a hike in the Guadalupes involves a special feeling. Usually the hour is early, because beginning any later means climbing in the heat. Stuff the sleeping bag, lace the hiking boots over clean wool socks, swing on the pack and check it for balance, tighten the shoulder and belt straps, and fill the canteens. Then, shortly before dawn, sign the register at the trailhead and trudge off on the gravelly trail. It's the same every time; yet it's different every time.

Guadalupe hikes are mountain hikes so the first part is uphill, unlike canyon hiking. To me most of the discomfort and tiredness happens soon after I start walking. Maybe I start out too fast, maybe it takes time to warm up; I resent the uphill grade and am surprised at how often I have to stop to sit under a juniper and catch my breath. But that feeling passes, it always does. Soon I warm up and settle into a slow pace that seems right for the grade of the trail.

Looking up can be intimidating. The long vertical distance looms up to the ridge tops and every inch of it will be gained by my own leg muscles, lifting me and my gear. But the rise is fast, and the flatlands drop away quickly. The tents in the campground become miniature spots of color in the grey-green of the lowland shrubs, with toy cars or vans nearby. The vegetation shows the altitude change. That grey-green around the campground is cactus, yucca, and the strange, beautiful Texas madrone trees. But going up the mountainside, that plant community soon disappears, replaced by juniper trees mostly, with a few scattered yucca. Though not very tall, the junipers give good shade for those rest stops.

Somewhere in the first few hours the hiker experiences one of the supreme pleasures of the desert: drinking water. One old man in the desert used to tell me: "The sun just sucks the sweat right out of you." It's easy to wait too long to take a drink. When you are thirsty, drink— don't carry the water in your canteen all day. I stop, take off my pack, and savor the view, a hundred miles of Texas spread out below, and sip from the canteen.

Coming over the rim at the top is an experience duplicated at few mountain ranges. The rim is a time-gate, and the hiker walks into a forest that belongs hundreds of miles north. The reason rests in the recent geologic history of the Guadalupes. Fifteen thousand years ago, when glaciers covered much of North America and the climate was cooler, a great forest came down over Colorado, New Mexico, and as far south as Texas. As the climate warmed, the forest retreated; or looked at another way, the desert advanced northward. But here, on an island high in the sky over the advancing desert, a piece of that great forest remains. There are Douglas-fir here and forest animals, even bear. The transition is startling.

CATHY J. RUDY

CATHY J. RUDY

The Guadalupe hiker lives in two worlds. He sees the details quietly taken in enroute to the top; then the exhilaration of the top and the forest in The Bowl (opposite).

Previous pages: View from trail on McKittrick Ridge.

The fierce uphill is over now and this part of the trip is what most hikers seek. The office, the preparations, the car, the highway, all those people down below become impossibly distant. In this rolling country, the forest sometimes encloses me; it may even seem cool. It is always silent. And on a trail that leads to a peak or along the rim, you can know what it is to be a bird soaring over the Texas desert. In every direction the land stretches away and never really stops. A fine lunch spot.

The afternoon hours are good ones. If there is a goal, I push on, but I prefer a leisurely hike with plenty of time for side trips and investigating special places. Late afternoon is a time to watch the sky. In July and August, especially, the afternoon thunderheads are impressive. It's a good time to be in a high place and just watch. Pick out a cloud; it is astonishing how it grows. Sometimes the drama of the storm becomes intense. If you are lucky, the rain may fall where you are, but usually it is just a tremendous show.

The afternoons blend into evening up here. I suddenly realize that the divisions of the day that seem so real down below, of leaving the office, commuting home, and listening to the evening news, are artificial. The day is a whole, undivided. Afternoon becomes evening. Evening becomes night. If it is the first night out in awhile, sleep does not come easily, but being awake is so fine I don't mind. The ground is hard, but after walking all day that is fine too. You shift position and look up at the sky slowly wheeling past the silhouettes of the trees. The stars move across the sky, at the same pace and for the same reason as the sun appears to move during the day. It's obvious but easy to miss if you only see the sky for a minute, walking between the restaurant and the car.

A good kind of tiredness comes on the second or third day of a hike. The pack has become familiar. I don't think about it much anymore, and its rhythmic creakings seem a friendly, natural accompaniment to the crunch of my footsteps. There is no need to think about the beginning or the end of the hike. Everything is working. I have plenty of water, and the aloneness is comfortable, nonthreatening. It is one of the few times when "now" is enough, not just a passage to something else.

Finally it is time to go back down again. On almost any trail in the Guadalupes the lip is obvious. With one step you are on top, with the next you are on the way down. Dormant muscles are in use, and even though it doesn't demand as much of my lungs as going up, I can get aches and quivers coming down. But overall it is easier and is one reason I prefer mountains to canyons. Now it is junipers again, and yucca, and pretty soon the desert flats.

Things seem to move faster now, and suddenly I am back. This may be the other very special moment, akin to starting a Guadalupe hike. I take off my pack and go over to the Park Service building to get a long, long drink of water. Even if I'm almost broke I treat myself that night to an extra good meal on the drive home. Without denial, the bath and bed are good. But there's something hollow about them too. Somehow the reality is back up there on top. Days later, on some "normal" day in the "normal" air-conditioned office . . . I remember.

Opposite: Near Pine Top backcountry campsite at dusk.

horned lizard

Cover photograph by George H. H. Huey
Back cover photograph by Cathy J. Rudy
Edited by Rose Houk

Geology consultation by Dr. Lloyd C. Pray
Coordinated by Bob Peters
Designed by Christina Watkins
Printed by Paragon Press, Inc.
Printed on Recycled Paper